An Old Timer's Travels Around the Isle of Man

– PAUL YATES –

An environmentally friendly book printed and bound in England by
www.printondemand-worldwide.com

This book is made entirely of chain-of-custody materials

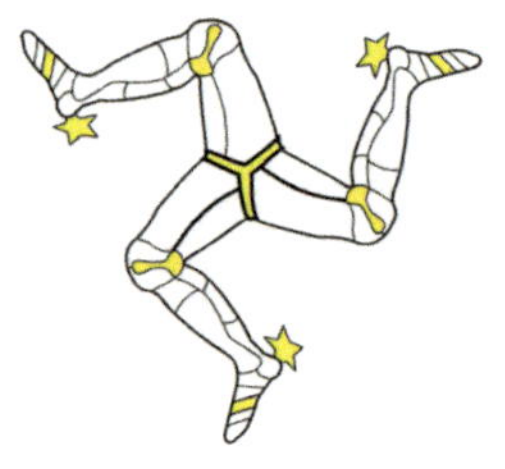

www.fast-print.net/store.php

AN OLD TIMER'S TRAVELS AROUND THE ISLE OF MAN

A catalogue record for this book is available from the British Library

ISBN 978-178035-658-7

First published 2013 by
FASTPRINT PUBLISHING
Peterborough, England.

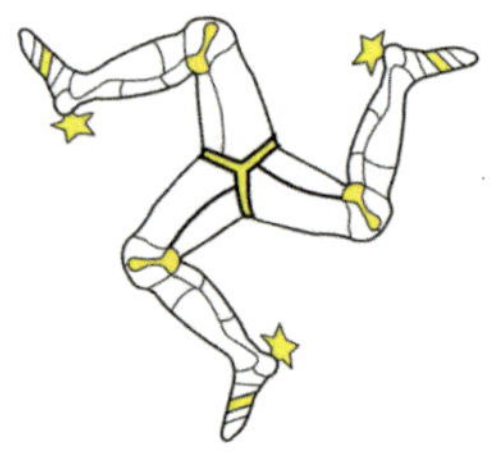

AN OLD TIMER'S TRAVELS AROUND THE ISLE OF MAN

– PAUL YATES –

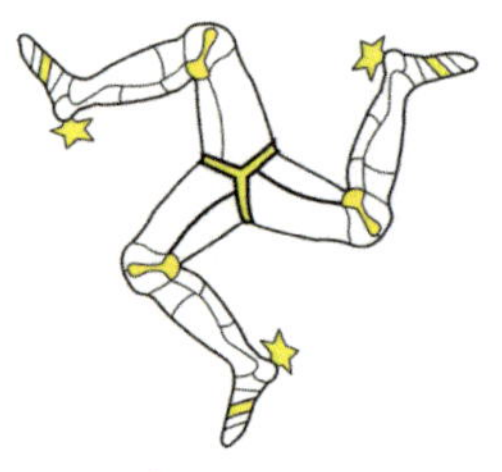

Contents

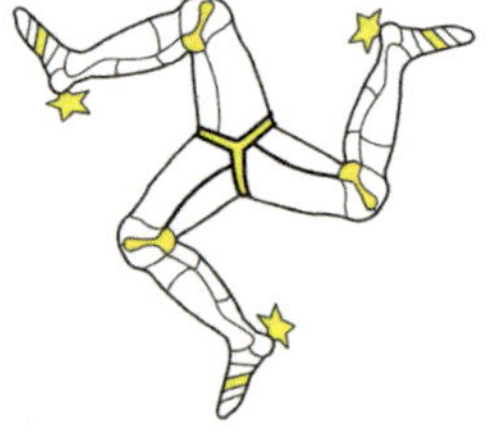

Preface

Over the last forty years I have been fortunate enough to travel around the world as an engineer in the aviation industry. I have many memories and plenty of photographs, but I have been rather short keeping a diary or journal.

With this in mind I decided that it was about time to revisit some of my favourite places and write about my travels. The philosophy behind my journeys is to visit as many places of interest and at a reasonably affordable cost. Towards this end I decided to use a bicycle, whenever possible, as a means of getting around. This does not preclude using other forms of transport, but is affordable, fun and healthy.

Hopefully, if an old timer like me can manage such travels on a bicycle, then most people can do the same, whether on two wheels or four wheels (or three wheels if you prefer).

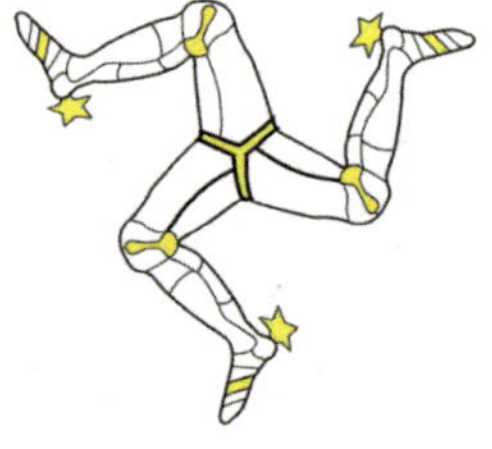

Foreword

**Foreword by Geoff Corkish MBE, MHK,
Isle of Man Political Member
with Responsibility for Tourism**

Dear Reader

The Isle of Man is the perfect place to visit all year round and can be quickly and easily reached by air or sea from a range of destinations across the UK.

Encompassing diverse, beautiful scenery, the island boasts a high quality of life, rugged coastlines, unspoilt beaches and lots of activities for all to enjoy in a safe and secure environment. There is also a wealth of cultural heritage sites to explore including one of the most well-preserved castles in Europe, Castle Rushen, and the imposing ancient castle and island fortress of Peel Castle.

The Isle of Man is an ideal location for visitors who want to experience the outdoor lifestyle or those looking for a relaxing break amid its tranquil shores. Together with quality accommodation and award winning local produce you'll soon see why the Isle of Man is a perfect visitor destination.

I would like to express my personal thanks to Paul Yates for taking the time to write this most informative and interesting book on his travels around the Isle of Man and I hope it will tempt you to visit soon.

If you would like more information on the Isle of Man, log on to www.visitisleofman.com or phone 01624 686766.

Yours sincerely

Geoff Corkish MBE, MHK

Acknowledgement

I would like to thank the Isle of Man Department of Tourism and Leisure, and Anna Hemy in particular, for all of their help in making my cycling holiday, and this book, possible. My thanks, also, go to them for supplying photographs for use in this book. Photographs are copyright of the Department of Tourism and Leisure, except were stated.

I wish to thank Paul and Sue Richards for their kind hospitality and offer of help, as well as their welcoming meal at the China Town restaurant on the day I arrived.

Also, my appreciation goes to all those I met on my 'adventure'; their help and hospitality were most kind and really appreciated.

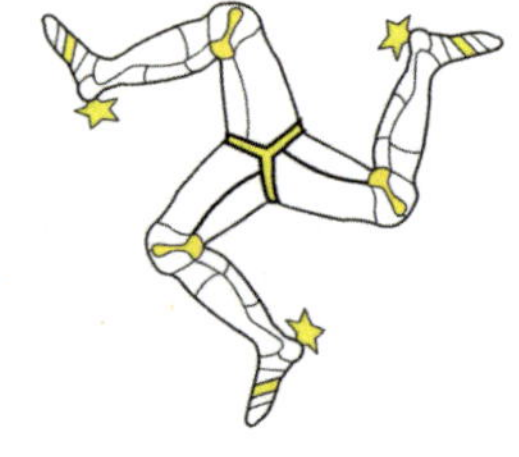

Dedication

This travelogue is dedicated to my late mother, Nancye Yates, who encouraged me to go on the cycling holiday, and to write about my adventures.

Also, I would like to dedicate this book to my wife, Pam and son, Ben for all their support and encouragement. (I am sure they appreciated the rest while I was away!)

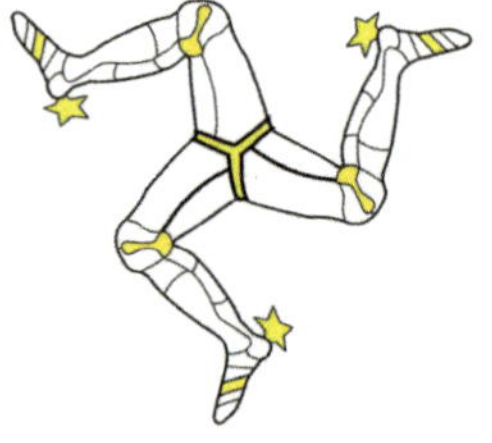

Introduction

The Lonely Planet's Guide[1] states the English "mainlanders have long suspected the Isle of Man… of being an odd place, full of weird island folk and their quirky ways…. Chances are that those same mainlanders have never actually seen the lush valleys, barren hills and rugged coastlines of what is a surprisingly beautiful island. Perfect for walking, cycling, driving or just relaxing, this is a place that doggedly refuses to sell itself down the river of crass commercialism and mass tourism."

"Home to the world's oldest continuous parliament, the Isle of Man enjoys special status in Britain, and its annual parliamentary ceremony honours the thousand year history of the Tynwald[2]."

With this in mind I wanted to find out for myself something of the history, nature and character of the Isle of Man. Hence, in early 2010, I searched the internet and web sites such as the Manx Tourist Office[3] for as much information as I could find.

Although the Isle of Man is part of the British Isles, it is a British protectorate with its own legislative council, language and culture. The Manx parliament was

---

[1] http://www.lonelyplanet.com/england/northwest-england/isle-of-man
[2] http://www.tynwald.org.im
[3] http://www.visitisleofman.com

established more than a thousand years ago by the Vikings who ruled the island at the time. However, it is more than just a part of history as, on 5 July every year, Tynwald assembles on Tynwald Hill, at St Johns village to read out, in Manx Gaelic and English, all the legislation enacted over the previous year. All Manx residents present have the right to petition the government on any point. This is a truly democratic process.

The Isle of Man has become famous for the T.T. (Tourist Trophy) motorcycle races, other motorsports such as the Manx Grand Prix and car rallies amongst others. If they are of interest, then you should, perhaps, make an effort to go during the times that they are on.

However life on the Isle of Man is, generally, a little slower and more relaxed than that to be found during the T.T. races. This suited me as I wanted time to relax and explore the island.

I had planned to cycle around the island, stopping at towns along the way. The route I came up with involved 10–15 miles each day, starting at Douglas, the main point of entry by sea and heading in a clockwise direction. This would allow me time to visit places of interest and to take care of any unplanned excursions or events.

I had chosen to take a folding bicycle with me, but cycle hire is available on the island. The machine is not really built for speed, endurance or comfort but can fold down to a relatively small size and be stored anywhere. A rear carrier and a set of pannier bags stored all my needs and wants. A spanner and a puncture repair kit, along with two spare inner tubes took up little space and would cover some possibilities. A cape should keep the rain off (most of me).

With my travels planned, and the ferry and hotels booked, I was ready to set forth. This book, then, is a brief narrative about my journey around the Isle of Man and the places I have visited.

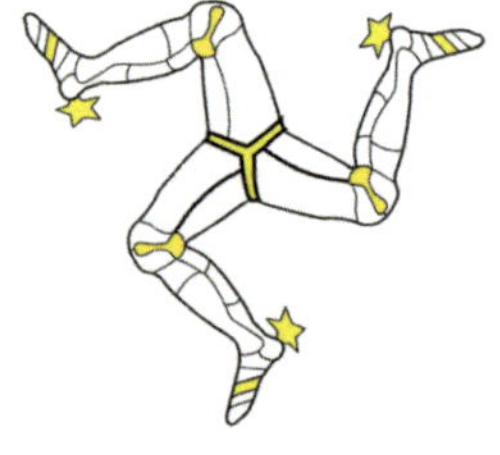

AN OLD TIMER'S TRAVELS AROUND THE ISLE OF MAN

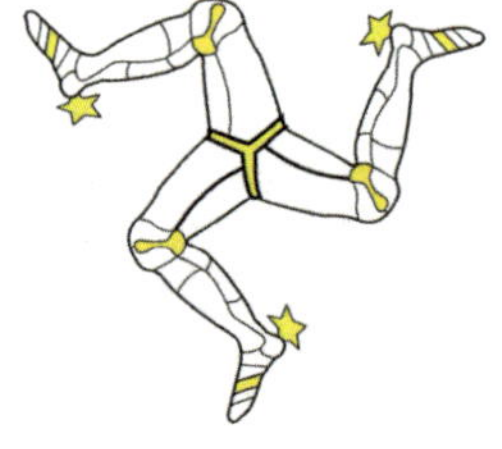

Day 1 - Liverpool/Douglas Saturday, 17 July 2010

I had travelled up to Liverpool on the previous evening and checked in at the Travelodge hotel on the Brunswick Dock. This had the advantage of having only two miles to travel to the Steam Packet sea terminal, close to the Royal Liver building. The journey from the hotel to the sea terminal went past the Albert Docks and the sight of some old sailing ships was a timely reminder of the city's maritime heritage. The water front, along with much of the city, was undergoing rejuvenation and the results that I could see were good.

The Isle of Man Steam Packet Company[4] has been providing sea services to the island for more than 175 years and, today, operates a fast catamaran from Liverpool to Douglas. The Manannan is a fairly recent acquisition and is larger than I would have imagined. There are four powerful engines and bow thrusters that allow careful manoeuvring in the harbours. The car deck has ample space for a large number of vehicles, and the passenger deck is similarly proportioned, with modern facilities. I had travelled from Liverpool to Douglas on many occasions, but I would have to say that this would be the most comfortable, and quickest, sailing I have ever been on.

---

[4] http://www.steam-packet.com

I arrived early at the sea terminal, but noted that there was already a queue of cars. Having a bicycle, I took the liberty of riding to the front of the queue of traffic waiting to board the ferry. A couple of motorcyclists had the same idea and soon joined me on the jetty. I knew that the ferry had been suffering technical troubles with one of the four engines, with repairs being undertaken while the vessel was in normal service to minimise disruption to the normal passenger timetable. Due to these technical problems, the ferry arrived a few minutes later than scheduled, but the arriving passengers and vehicles were off-loaded promptly and departing passengers boarded with the least delay.

I rode up the ramp and parked my bicycle on the side, close to the entrance. I was, I suppose, being a little lazy in not moving further down the deck, but I knew that the corner, by the ramp, would not be needed by any of the larger vehicles and it would allow me to make a quick exit at the other end of the journey. Soon, I was making my way up to the passenger deck and ordered breakfast. I found the passenger area spacious and comfortable. Towards the front is a large seating area with an excellent view ahead of the vessel. Nearby is a café and seating area where it is possible to buy drinks, snacks and meals; a little further back is a shop with a reasonable supply of books, magazines, drinks and souvenirs of the voyage.

I avoided the bar at the rear of the passenger deck and made do with a big breakfast and a cup of tea. Eventually I settled down with a couple of magazines. The 2½ hours, or so, that it took to cross the Irish Sea went past very quickly, and I was pleased to see Douglas Bay when it slipped into view.

When the vehicle deck was opened, I headed for my bicycle and made ready for disembarkation. With the lowering of the ramp, safety checks had to be carried out prior to allowing the vehicles to disembark. In that short space of time I felt a sense of excitement at the thought of my holiday actually starting. However, I felt a certain dread. My adventure was about to begin and I had to face all that my journey would throw at me. There was no turning back now.

Very soon we were allowed to continue and I rode up along the jetty, as quickly as I could, and followed the directions onto the Loch Promenade, passing the rows of vehicles waiting to board the ferry for the return trip. It did not take the disembarking cars long to catch up, but I was able to continue at a leisurely pace, keeping a careful eye on the traffic and pedestrians making their way to their hotels.

I managed to cycle past the Ellan Vannin hotel, where I should be staying for the first night, but, having realised my mistake, I simply dismounted and turned around, then pushed my bicycle back along the footpath. Outside the hotel I folded my bike and stowed it inside the bag, before carrying it, and the panniers, up the steps to the reception area.

Although the manager was busy checking in the guests who had arrived on the ferry, he made time to welcome me and ask about my visit to the Isle of Man. I explained that I would be cycling around the island and that I would be staying for one night only at the start, and two nights at the end. Also, it would be handy if I could pay for the three nights stay at that point; that would save having to settle the bill later. That was done and dusted. I asked if there was anywhere I could store my bicycle overnight. As it was folded up and in its bag, it was suggested that I could leave it in the guest lounge area of the hotel as it would not take up much space and the room was not being used much. I deposited the remainder of my possessions in my room.

As I had completed check-in at the hotel, I decided I had time to visit the Manx Museum[5] on Kingswood Grove. The walk up the short, steep hill was a bit of an effort, but well worth the trouble. It has to be said that driving a car would have meant that I could have taken the easier, but longer route. The introductory film was very informative and well presented, as were the exhibition halls that cover Manx history and geography from the earliest times to the present. The Manx Museum begins to tell the "Story Of Mann" that continues around the island.

That evening I took a ride on the Douglas Horse Trams[6] to the northern end of the Douglas Promenade. It was there that I went for a meal at the China Town restaurant with Paul and Sue Richard and their family. I had made contact with them through Mensa prior to making my journey to the Isle of Man. Their company and hospitality were most welcome, and it seemed most reassuring to know that there are genuine people who really care. I returned to my hotel safe in the knowledge that a friendly voice, or help, was only a telephone call away.

---

[5] http://www.visitisleofman.com/placestovisit/museums/manx.xml

[6] http://www.visitisleofman.com/thingstoseeanddo/railways/horsetrams/xml

A gentle stroll along the promenade helped work off the meal and left me in a relaxed frame of mind by the time I got back to the hotel. That ensured a good night's sleep.

Day 2 - Douglas/Ballasalla/Castletown Sunday, 18 July 2010

The Sunday was my first full day on the Isle of Man and I had a full Manx breakfast before making an early start, heading south towards Ballasalla and Castletown. Being on a bicycle, I had time to enjoy the countryside that I found to be idyllic and peaceful.

The weather was a little overcast with occasional light drizzle, but that did not bother me. My route took me round the inner harbour in Douglas and passed the Old Nunnery, before going under the steam railway bridge. Very soon I was on the main road heading south towards Castletown. It was on this stretch of road I passed the rest home for retired horses. Sadly it was not open to the public at the time I was there, but I thought it was nice to know that the horses are looked after when they have finished their working lives on the Douglas horse trams or wherever it may be.

It was on the Douglas to Castletown road that I came across one piece of Celtic culture and mythology that can be found on the Isle of Man. This instance concerns the Fairy Bridgewhere, locals will tell you, you should greet "the little people"; if you don't, then something bad will happen. I, obviously, incurred the displeasure of "the little people" as I picked up two punctures in the back tyre of my bicycle. More about this later.

I have travelled along this road many times, and I had always thought that it was fairly level. However, at one point I was freewheeling downhill and was surprised to see that I was doing 26mph. This was not fast for some of the top racing cyclists, but it was rather unnerving for an old timer, especially as conditions were a little damp and my glasses were misting up with the drizzle.

Anyway, my journey continued to the village of Ballasalla and Rushen Abbey[7]. Although these have been no more than ruins since the dissolution of the monasteries, the abbey is still an intriguing place and recent excavations have thrown light on life so long ago. The work of the Manx National Heritage has produced a place that should be of interest to most people. However, the abbey has been put to many uses over the years, including serving cream teas and entertainment for visitors.

Nearby is Silverdale Glen[8], one of 17 beautiful glens on the island. It is on the footpath that runs through the glen that can be found Monk's Bridge, which was built to allow the crossing of the stream, particularly while carrying goods to and from the abbey.

From the car park close to Rushen Abbey it is possible to turn right and drive through a ford in the Silverburn River, providing the water is not too high. Being on a bicycle I decided to take the alternative route, around the back of the abbey and through the village.

Just two or three miles further south from Ballasalla is Castletown, the ancient capital of Mann. The town and

---

[7] http://www.visitisleofman.com/placestovisit/heritage/rushenabbey.xml

[8] http://www.visitisleofman.com/placestovisit/parks/silverdale.xml

harbour are dominated by Castle Rushen[9], one of the best preserved medieval castles in Europe. Fortifications were established here during the Viking era and expanded during Scottish and English rule. In later years, the castle saw a number of uses before being handed over to the Manx National Heritage who completed restoration of the building.

The entrance to the castle is along a pathway over which the moat would have been, and through the arched entrance with a magnificent portcullis. It is very easy to imagine how imposing the castle must have been in medieval times, as it still is.

Once through the main entrance of the outer defences, or "curtain wall" there is a large courtyard surrounding the inner defences or keep. At one time this part of the castle would have been surrounded by a second moat and access would have been via a drawbridge. The pathway continues through the original entrance with its original double portcullises. Any invading forces trapped between the two defences would have been dealt with from access holes in the roof above.

Inside the keep it is possible to follow a route that would take you to the highest ramparts, from where you can gain a magnificent view of the town and surrounding area. However, I decided to stay with the lower levels which are set out to tell the history of the castle. Most of the rooms have been laid out to represent different times throughout history.

Near Castle Rushen, on the opposite side of Castle

---

[9] http://www.visitisleofman.com/placestovisit/heritage.castlerushen.xml

Street, is the Old House of Keys[10]. This was the home of the Manx parliament, Tynwald, until Douglas took over from Castletown as the capital of the Isle of Man in 1874. One of the attractions here is to sit in the chamber, with other visitors, and debate topics of importance throughout the island's history.

Prior to this building being used by Tynwald, there were a number of other buildings that were used as meeting places for the legislative council. One of them was the George Hotel where I would be staying that evening.

Close to the Old House of Keys is the Old Grammar School[11]. This one-time church is the oldest roofed building on the island. When the school closed in the early 20th century, it was left as it was and turned into a museum. It was as I left for the hotel that I discovered the first of the punctures on the back wheel of my bicycle. However, I decided to leave the repairs till the following morning.

One thing I had not considered in planning my holiday was the fact that some restaurants and cafés close for one day a week, and this varies from place to place. In Castletown it is Sunday evening. Although the bar in the George Hotel is open during the evening, food is only served during the day. Sadly most of the other restaurants were closed, but I managed to get a meal at The Viking Hotel Restaurant in Station Road.

---

[10] http://www.visitisleofman.com/placestovisit/heritage/oldhouseofkeys.xml

[11] http://www.visitisleofman.com/placestovisit/heritage/oldgrammarschool.xml

Back at the George Hotel I enjoyed a pint of beer with a group of locals who were in the bar. The company was friendly and welcoming. Eventually, I turned in for the night and had a most comfortable sleep.

Day 3 - Castletown/Cregneash/ Port Erin Monday, 19 July 2010

I came down for breakfast at 8:30 to find that I had been the only resident. I was more than a little surprised as I had rated the hotel very highly.

Anyway, I checked out from the hotel and headed to the Nautical Museum[12], by the harbour. This magnificent establishment is based around the 17th century yacht *Peggy* that was discovered in 1935, bricked up, in the basement. The boat was, allegedly, used for smuggling, amongst other activities. The museum, opened in 1951, covers many areas of maritime history associated with the Isle of Man.

After leaving the Nautical Museum I made my way to a local garage for help with the puncture on the rear wheel of my bike. The main problem was that the spanners I had were not up to undoing the wheel nuts, as they had been tightened up too much. Anyway, with the wheel out I changed the inner tube and checked the tyre for the cause of the puncture; no sign of the problem.

Soon enough, I was on my way to Cregneash village; my route took in the Castletown bypass and part of the

---

[12] http://www.visitisleofman.com/placestovisit/museums/nautical.xml

Southern 100 race circuit. As racing is held on closed public roads, I was glad I had chosen a quieter period. Not that it bothered me, but I could not see how to make my way south without going on a long detour. However, on the way to Port St Mary my exuberance was dampened by a second puncture in the rear tyre. As the road up to Cregneash is rather steep, I decided to walk and enjoy the view.

Slowly, the scenery changed from one of a lush, agricultural background to a higher ground with gorse and bracken. The climb was steep, but not insurmountable. However, the reward was worth the effort.

Cregneash[13] is an old crofters' village that has been turned into the island's national folk museum. Many of the buildings have thatched roofs and whitewashed walls. Visitors can find information about the village at the ticket office. Upstairs from the ticket office is an exhibition about the history of the village. In the same building is the Cregneash Tea Room where cream teas are served. Many of the staff are dressed in period costume and add authenticity to the folk museum.

Many of the places to be found here are, or were, the homes of people who worked the land, which have been preserved as they would have been more than a century ago. One of the first cottages to be given to the Manx National Heritage was owned by Harry Kelly, one of the last native Manx speakers.

Other attractions include a smithy and a wood-

[13] http://www.visitisleofman.com/placestovisit/heritage/cregneash/xml

turners workshop. During the summer there are demonstrations of spinning and weaving. Also there are exhibits relating to the agricultural life that would have been found in, and around, the village. Part of the village church, at one time, was also used as a school for the children of the area.

Just south of Cregneash is the Sound Visitor Centre[14] that overlooks the Calf Sound, a short stretch of water between the main island and the Calf of Man. The Calf is, usually, uninhabited and is used as a bird sanctuary, although it would have been farmed at one time.

Heading north-west, I followed a small country lane down to Port Erin. There was minimal traffic on this road and the solitude, along with the rugged terrain, seemed to add to the tranquillity of my journey. However, the descent into Port Erin was short-lived and I soon found the Anchorage Guest House. This accommodation, like the Ellan Vannin hotel in Douglas, reminded me of the older style of terraced hotel with a number of levels.

I had a bit of spare time before places started closing for the day, and I paid a quick visit to the Railway Museum[15] next to the steam railway terminus. Although it is not that big, the exhibition was large enough to give a marvellous insight into the heyday of this Victorian transport system.

From the railway museum, I went in search of something to eat. My previous evening's experience was to be repeated as many of the restaurants in Port Erin are

---

[14] http://www.visitisleofman.com/placestovisit/natureandbeauty/soundandcalfofman.xml
[15] http://www.visitisleofman.com/plavestovisit/museums/railway.xml

closed on a Monday evening. However I walked down towards the promenade and found the Falcon's Nest hotel. Being hungry, and thirsty, I called in for a drink and an evening meal. The bar had quite a few customers enjoying the hostelry and I found the atmosphere very friendly. I had almost finished my meal when a group of young people came in and sat on adjacent tables. They were soon joined by others. As I had finished my meal I moved to the bar to give them more room. I received a very polite 'thank you' for giving them a little more room.

Back at the hotel I met a couple who were staying there. They came from Darwen, near Blackburn, which was coincidental as a family relative lives in the town. I could not help thinking that it is a small world.

Before turning in, I repaired the puncture to the original inner tube. That was a task I had not carried out for more than forty years, but was able to complete fairly quickly.

Day 4 - Port Erin/Peel Tuesday, 20 July 2010

After breakfast I replaced the rear inner tube and, after closer inspection, found the cause of the punctures; a small staple had become lodged in the tyre and only came through the tyre wall when I was riding the bike. Such is life. As I mentioned previously, I had not repaired a puncture for many years and I felt a little unsure that I would do a good enough job, but the repair was good and held out for the remainder of my journey. Also, I did feel a little uneasy as I was certain that the local residents would object to me carrying out running repairs on my bicycle, using the pavement as a workshop, but there were no complaints.

Back on the road, I was heading northwards to Peel. My route took me inland, before turning left towards the sea once again, and close to the beautiful Niarbyl Bay. Although the road was a little hillier than I had been used to on the first two days, my efforts were well rewarded as the countryside and views were magnificent. Also, the weather turned out to very nice. In fact, I picked up a bit of a suntan.

Just before arriving in Peel, I turned inland and took a detour to the village of St. Johns. It is here that Tynwald

Hill[16] is to be found. This iconic landmark is of great importance in Manx culture, history and politics as it is here that the Manx Parliament meets on 5 July every year to read out all the new laws. This ceremony has its roots in the original legislative council that was set up by the Viking Kings of Mann more than a thousand years ago. Nearby is the Chapel of St John where a service is held before the procession proceeds to Tynwald Hill. A little further afield is the Tynwald Museum that displays a pictorial history of the events.

On the other side of the main road I found a very nice café; I cannot remember the name, but it may have been the Tynwald Café. The service was fine and the food was delicious. The one thing that stuck in my mind was a long table or bench with four stools with padded seats on top of what looked like a pair of ladies' legs, wearing stockings and a short skirt at the top. Hence, anybody sitting on the stools would look as though they had rather curvaceous legs. Not so good for the macho man!

From St. Johns village, I headed west to Peel, known locally as 'Sun Set City'. This town has a magnificent harbour that is dominated by Peel Castle perched on St. Patrick's Isle. I spent part of the evening watching a beautiful sunset amid peaceful tranquillity.

However, before enjoying the evening in Peel, I visited an intriguing museum, the House of Manannan[17] This continues the 'Story Of Mann' that begins in the Manx Museum in Douglas. There are a number of films

---

[16] http://www.visitisleofman.com/placestovisit/heritage/tynwaldhill.xml
[17] http://www.visitisleofman.com/placestovisit/heritage/houseofmanannan.xml

and a host of excellent displays. In fact, the introductory film was one of the best pieces I have ever seen and featured the Celtic Sea God, Manannan. There are many interactive displays and I could have spent much more time there. The museum had won an award as Museum of the Year.

One of the last exhibits that I came across was a replica Viking longboat *Odin's Raven* that was built in Norway and sailed to the Isle of Man in 1979 to commemorate the millennium year of the Manx Parliament, Tynwald, that was established by the Vikings.

I first saw this longboat in 1985 when I visited the island with my wife for the first time. At the time there was a gentleman dressed as a Viking warrior and he used to pose with the tourists. I got my camera out to take a photograph of my wife standing next to him. Just as I took the picture this 'Viking' said that he was going to go out raping and pillaging, but would leave the pillaging to later. It was not until a few weeks later, that I was showing the pictures to some of the people I worked with that one of the women said that the woman in the background of the shot was her sister. Another coincidence!

I managed to find a very good restaurant, the Creek Inn, that seemed to be very popular and served excellent food. Having been well fed and watered, I checked in at the Waldick Hotel at the northern end of the promenade.

Day 5 - Peel/Ramsey Wednesday, 21 July 2010

As I had not managed to see all I wanted to in Peel, I delayed my departure from this pleasant and picturesque town. The first place to visit was Peel Castle[18] on St Patrick's Isle. The location was ideal from a defensive point of view and the massive curtain wall would have deterred most attacking forces. In fact, fortifications have been here for many centuries and there is a lot of history involved with the area.

While the outer wall is intact, many of the buildings within these ramparts have fallen into disrepair. However, on a nice day it is possible to spend a pleasant hour or two wandering around the castle grounds, listening to the audio guide.

As with many places on the Isle of Man, there are many legends to be found in Peel. One concerns the Black Dog of Peel that took up residence in the castle. For the interest of the visitor, there is a model of the Black Dog of Peel near the entrance to the castle. Later in the day I telephoned my family and I told my son that I had seen the Black Dog. By coincidence, as I spoke, a dog started barking in a garden nearby. My son was mortified

[18] http://www.visitisleofman.com/placestovisit/heritage/peelcastle.xml

as he thought that I had been attacked by a spectral hound!

Anyway, I retraced my route around the harbour, first stopping at Moore's Traditional Kippers[19], one of the last genuine kipper factories on the island that still uses oak chips to smoke the herring, and then visited the Manx Transportation Museum[20]. This is a rather small establishment, located in the office of the former brick works, but has several exhibits, including the Peel P.50, probably the world's smallest production car.

Finally I visited the Leece Museum[21] that displays many items related to the history of Peel.

My journey continued northwards, along the coast, towards Ramsey. At Kirk Michael my route joined the famous T.T. (Tourist Trophy) Mountain Circuit. Although I was riding along at a leisurely 10mph, I tried to imagine what it would be like travelling at more than 150mph.

At the entrance to Ballaugh village, I noticed a farm produce shop that sold cream teas, etc. I had remembered that my hosts of the previous Saturday had mentioned such a place. It turned out that this was the right establishment and is known locally as Halcyon Days. Sadly, there was nobody else in the café when I arrived, but I was served afternoon tea and scones and enjoyed a pleasant conversation with the lady who ran the business.

I had been there for quite a while when another

---

[19] http://www.manxkippers.com
[20] http://www.visitisleofman.com/placestovisit/museums/manxtransport/xml
[21] http://www.visitisleofman.com/placestovisit/museums/leece.xml

cyclist arrived. This turned out to be a young lady from Port Erin who was making the best of the good weather and was riding around the northern part of the island. This lady did complain that her husband/partner had preferred to stay at home, rather than accompany her on her travels.

Initially, I do not think that she realised that I had arrived by bicycle. I pointed out that my transport was parked by the entrance. Although she had seen it, she thought it had been left there to attract customers.

From Ballaugh I followed the T.T. course to Sulby village and the Sulby Glen Hotel[22]. This is one of the well-known and much-liked vantage points during the T.T. races, but no high-speed road racing today. I found the Sulby Glen Hotel to be a very friendly and warm place, with very helpful staff. I had arrived in the late afternoon and had the bar to myself for a little while I talked to the person running the place. When engaged in conversation, the telephone rang. All I heard was, "Yes… he is here with me now…"

Looking at me the barman said "It's your wife".

I then had to explain what I was doing in the bar and that I was not getting drunk. Having said that, the weather had been warm and sunny, and I was in need of a refreshing drink.

Later in the evening there were a lot more customers and a lively atmosphere. I got talking to two gentlemen, who were there with their families; they came from Nottinghamshire. I was surprised to find out that they

[22] http://www.sulbyglen.net/

knew the small, rural village of Ossington where my mother was born in 1919.

They recommended the chicken curry that was on the bar menu. This particular dish is a favourite of my son and myself, so I had to indulge myself in honour of my son back home. With that I turned in and had a good night's sleep.

Day 6 - Ramsey/Laxey Thursday, 22 July 2010

After a good breakfast, I was on my way to Ramsey and the Grove Rural Life Museum[23]. This building was once the home of a wealthy Liverpool businessman and, after the passing of his three daughters, was given to the Manx National Heritage as a reminder of rural life in Victorian times. Apart from the displays of domestic life, there is much on show relating to rural and farming life. Also, I came across some Loaghtan sheep that are native to the Isle of Man.

Ramsey is the northern terminus of the Manx Electric Railway that follows the east coast to Laxey and Douglas. Although I had intended riding all around the island, and the next section was not too hilly, I succumbed to temptation and took the train. The view around Maughold Head was magnificent with a view of the rugged coastline in the distance.

Arriving at Laxey, I climbed down from the train and retrieved my bicycle that was folded up in its bag. As I did so I took no notice of several groups of people sitting around, enjoying the sun and a cool drink. Anyway, I opened the bike bag, extricated the bike and restored it to its normal operating mode; the bike bag was then folded

---

[23] http://www.visitisleofman.com/placestovisit/museums.grove.xml

up to a small size and placed on the rear luggage rack. I was rather amused by a couple nearby who thought my antics were part of a magic act or a candid camera set up. This turned out to be an ice breaker and I was able to tell them of my journey around the island.

I soon found the B&B that I had booked for the evening. The Greaves was fairly high up on the side of the Laxey valley with a very pleasing view of the surrounding area.

I spent some of the late afternoon looking around the Laxey Wheel and Mines Trail[24]. Laxey was, for many years, a productive and profitable lead mine, and the Lady Isabella water wheel was built to pump water from the mine shafts that extended under sea level. At 72½ feet in diameter, this is the largest working wheel in the world, and still turns for the summer visitor. For the energetic, it is possible to climb the stairs to the top of the tower and look over the valley below.

During the summer, water is gravity-fed from the surrounding hills to the top of the tower and turns the massive wheel. The crank, in turn, operates a set of linkages and a beam that is connected to the water pump at the head of the mine shaft.

A path alongside the wheel takes the visitor to the mine entrance, where it is possible to walk the first few yards of the underground working. A hard hat is a necessity.

A road leads down the valley to Laxey harbour and I know that a trip down there is well worth the effort.

---

[24] http://www.visitisleofman.com/placestovisit/heritage/laxeywheel.xml

However, I was tiring and did not look forward to the climb back up the hill.

On the way back to my accommodation for the evening, I stopped for a very nice supper of fish and chips. Before settling in for the night I wrote up a few notes about my travels, as I looked out at the setting sun across the valley. I could not have wished for a better view.

Day 7 - Laxey/Douglas Friday, 23 July 2010

During breakfast I became engaged in conversation with one of the six guests staying at the guest house. I can't remember his name, but I know he was a teacher and he was intrigued by my travels round the island. I did try to explain that by the time I got to Ramsey I had been tiring and succumbed to temptation and took the train to Laxey. However, he did not want to hear that as he wanted to think that I had made the effort to cycle around the island. It was later that I wondered if he wanted to use my story as an example for his pupils, of what can be done if you put your mind to it. Who knows?

I could not leave the village of Laxey without taking the Snaefell Mountain Railway to the highest point on the island. The railway was constructed soon after the electric railway from Douglas to Laxey was completed. The steady climb provides a wonderful view of the Laxey valley before crossing the Mountain Road and curling around Snaefell to reach the summit at 2,000 feet. At the terminus I stopped for a cup of tea at the café, before climbing to the highest point on the Isle of Man at 2,036 feet. It is from here that the Manx proudly claim to be able to see seven kingdoms: Mann, England, Scotland, Wales, Ireland, Manannan (the Celtic Sea God), and the

Kingdom of God.

After spending some time admiring the panoramic views from Snaefell, I returned to sea level on the mountain railway. After a final look around Laxey, I headed southwards to Douglas. Having followed the main road for a few miles, I turned left to head towards the coastline again. This road passes Groudle Glen, home of a magnificent narrow gauge railway that runs down to the sea. At one time it was possible for tourists to visit sea lions and polar bears that were on display in the bay. The animals that were kept here were returned to the wild in 1939.

Sadly, this railway line was not open on the day I came past, so I continued my travels along the coast road and enjoyed the picturesque scenery and tranquillity. However, it was not long before I met a retired police officer who was out walking his dog. We passed the time of day and spent some time in deep conversation. As always, it was pleasant to hear the views of others, particularly residents of the island.

After an enjoyable ride along the coastal road, I rounded Onchan Head and marvelled at Douglas Bay spread out below me. I was filled with a sense of satisfaction that I had virtually completed my journey and that I was on the final downhill stretch. However, I felt a certain sense of sadness that my travels were almost over. I freewheeled down to the promenade and followed the cycle track back to the Loch Promenade.

Later in the day, while in Douglas, I was in a photography shop and was most surprised to see the gentleman that I had spoken to in the hotel. He was passing and, having seen me in the shop, wanted to introduce his friend, who had just arrived on the island, to this adventurous old timer. I was rather flattered by the attention, but at a loss as to why anybody should see me as anything other than an eccentric old cyclist.

While I was in the photography shop I was dismayed to find one of the pictures on the camera's memory card had become corrupt and I was unable to download more than half of the photographs. Even the staff in the shop could not help. However, some two or three weeks later, I was talking to a nephew who is into photography, as well as working in the printing trade, and he was able to rescue all the photographs.

It was while walking through the main shopping area, looking for somewhere to eat, that I overheard a young man talking on his mobile telephone. Normally I avoid eavesdropping on people's private conversations, but on this occasion it was rather difficult, as the person concerned was not bothered who heard what was said. However, the point he was trying to put across to the other person was that he could not understand why anybody would want to "live in a dump like this". I thought that it would have been inappropriate to say anything, but, for me, the Isle of Man is somewhere where I would like to live, and is far better than some places where I have worked.

However, we are all entitled to our own opinions and, in a free society, we should be able to express those opinions. However, I felt that the remarks were in stark contrast to how I felt about the Isle of Man, particularly after a wonderful week of cycling around the island.

After my evening meal, and a reflection on my day's travels, I turned in for a restful night's sleep.

Day 8 - Douglas
Saturday, 24 July 2010

The Saturday was to be a relaxing day, taking in one or two places that I had missed when I first arrived on the island. My first stop was the Gaiety Theatre. Productions are a regular feature of this fine old building and, on Saturday mornings, it is possible to have a guided tour of the establishment, including backstage and understage areas.

From the Gaiety Theatre[25] I wandered through the main shopping centre and headed towards the north quay of the inner harbour. I was pleased to find an open air market, with live music, that seemed to be rather characteristic of the Isle of Man.

From the harbour, I followed the road up onto Douglas Head and to the Camera Obscura[26]. This is a very good example of a piece of Victorian Engineering. Most camera obscuras have a single lens and mirror in the roof to project a picture of an outside scene onto a table. In the case of the one in Douglas there are 12 lenses and mirrors that project all-around views onto the table.

---

[25] http://www.visitisleofman/thingstoseeanddo/artsculture/gaiety.xml
[26] http://www.visitisleofman/placestovisit/heritage/cameraobscura.xml

Sadly, my visit became a victim of misty conditions and inclement weather. The Camera Obscura had closed for the day as it would not have been possible to see the building at its best, and there would not have been many visitors.

I climbed down the side of what was the Douglas Head Incline Railway and to the harbour. On my way back to the Loch Promenade I saw the remains of the Solway Harvester. This fishing vessel sank in the Irish Sea a few years previously and had been brought to Douglas Harbour, waiting for an inquest into the accident. I found this a sad reminder of the harsh realities of life at sea.

Unrelated to this tragic event, but still connected to problems with sea travel in the past, is the Tower of Refuge in Douglas Bay, not too far from the outer harbour. As its name implies, it was built, in 1832, as a place of refuge for any sailors who had the misfortune to lose their vessels as they tried to enter Douglas harbour, particularly during stormy weather.

Sir William Hilary was involved with the funding of the Tower of Refuge, as well founding the RNLI lifeboats. As a result of that and technological advances, safety at sea is far better these days and the Tower of Refuge has not been needed for a long time.

In the late afternoon I made my way along the promenade and then up Broadway and Balla Quayle Road to Glencrutchery Road. Just a short distance along this road, to the right, is the start and finish line of the world famous T.T. motorcycle races. It was all quite peaceful while I was there – the only sound of racing machines was in my mind, as I tried to imagine the excitement of these annual events.

That evening I returned to the inner harbour, looking for somewhere to eat. Eventually, as I headed back towards the centre of town, I came across The Chart Room, a first class fish-and-chip shop, with ample seating. My cod and chips were most welcome.

Day 9 - Douglas/Liverpool
Sunday, 25 July 2010

My holiday on the Isle ofMan had reached an end. My alarm went off at 05:00, I clambered out of bed, dressed and packed my pannier bags for the last time. The only 'senior moment' I had was forgetting to pick up my crash helmet. I had placed it on top of the wardrobe and, being out of sight, I forgot all about it until I had left the hotel and shut the front door behind me. Having a short journey from the hotel to the sea terminal, I arrived on the early side, but made good use of my time.

Having checked in for the 07:00 sailing, I took my bicycle to the jetty, in readiness for boarding. Before long, I was allowed to ride down to (and up) the ramp, and tie my bike to the side wall. On the passenger deck I had a last view of Douglas as the ferry set sail. I was filled with a sense of sadness as I watched Douglas Bay disappear into the distance. I had really enjoyed my holiday and the challenge for cycling around the island. Over the next 2½ hours I had breakfast and wrote a few notes about my travels.

Back in Liverpool, I was able to disembark early and headed for the Lime Street Station. I was back to reality, home and work. Holidays can't last for ever, but the memories last longer.

Then it was down to work and write about my holiday. It has taken me six or seven attempts to write this book, but perseverance paid off and here it is, for what it is worth.

Post Script

Having cycled around the Isle of Man, I have to agree with the comments on the Lonely Planet's website. This is a beautiful island with a wealth of history and culture, and it has not given in to crass commercialism and mass tourism. There seems to be a unique identity to this wonderful island, an island that will not be rushed in the modern world.

The Lonely Planet website did suggest that "Douglas, the capital, is a run-down relic of Victorian tourism with fading B&Bs". While some of the hotels and B&Bs have closed and been turned into apartments, I felt that the town still retains much of the charming façade of the Victorian era, but has come into the 21st century in its own inimitable style.

The Isle of Man is certainly popular with those that visit every year, many from far afield; but I was left with a feeling that this island remains an unknown entity for many. Certainly, most will have heard of the T.T. races, tailless Manx cats and Manx kippers, but there is so much more to be discovered, as I found out for myself. Perhaps this really is a hidden gem waiting to be discovered.

Would I go back? Yes! Would I go by bicycle again? Probably! Although, at my age, assistance from an electric motor would be appreciated. Next time it would be nice to have a TV camera to record the sights and sounds, so other could see what the Isle of Man is really like. Then again... perhaps I should return to enjoy what the Isle of Man has to offer and seek those places I have missed.

I hope that, in some small way, you have enjoyed reading this short narrative and that, one day, you may find time to explore this wonderful island.

Paul Yates.

Photographs

Figure 1 - Douglas Horse Tram

Figure 2 - Manx Museum

Figure 3 - Castle Rushen (DoTL)

Figure 4 - Nautical Museum (DoTL)

Figure 5 - Cregneash Village (DoTL)

Figure 6 - The Road to the Calf of Man (DoTL)

Figure 7 - Calf Sound Visitor Centre (DoTL)

Figure 8 - Niarbyl Bay (DoTL)

Figure 9 - Peel Castle

Figure 10 - House of Manannan (DoTL)

Figure 11 - Grove Rural Life Museum (DoTL)

Figure 12 - Snaefell Mountain Railway (DoTL)

Figure 13 - Laxey Wheel

Figure 14 – Chapel of St John (next to Tynwald Hill)

Figure 15 – Fairy Bridge

Figure 16 – Ferry at Liverpool

Figure 17 – Inside Harry Kellys Cottage, Cregneash

Figure 18 – Loaghtan Sheep (Manx Museum)

Figure 19 – Manx Electric Railway

Figure 20 – Nautical Museum

Figure 21 – Norman Wisdom statue in Douglas

Figure 22 – The Old Grammar School

Figure 23 – Railway Museum

Figure 24 – Port Erin Station

Figure 25 – Sulby Glen Hotel

Bibliography

Manx National Heritage. (2010). *Castle Rushen Souvenir Booklet.* Douglas, Isle Of Man: Manx National Heritage.

Manx National Heritage. (2010). *Discover The Story Of Mann.* Douglas, Isle Of Man: Manx National Heritage.

Manx National Heritage. (2010). *House Of Manannan Souvenir Guide.* Douglas, Isle Of Man: Manx National Heritage.

Manx National Heritage. (2010). *National Folk Museum Cregneash Souvenir Booklet & Site Guide.* Douglas, Isle Of Man: Manx National Heritage.

Manx National Heritage. (2010). *Peel Castle Souvenir Booklet.* Douglas, Isle Of Man: Manx National Heritage.

Manx National Heritage. (2010). *Rushen Abbey Souvenier Booklet & Site Guide.* Douglas, Isle Of Man: Manx National Heritage.

Manx National Heritage. (2010). *The Gibbs Of The Grove Souvenir Booklet.* Douglas, Isle Of Man: Manx National Heritage.

Manx National Heritage. (2010). *The Nautical Museum Souvenir Booklet.* Douglas, Isle Of Man: Manx

National Heritage.

Manx National Heritage. (2010). *The Old House Of Keys Souvenir Booklet.* Douglas, Isle Of Man: Manx National Trust.

Manx National Herritage. (2010). *The Great Laxey Wheel & Mines Trail.* Douglas, Isle Of Man: Manx National Trust.

Travel Expenditure

The following costs are what I had to pay at the time and were, quite often, pre-booked to get discounted prices.

Transport

Date	**From**	**To**	**Operator**	**Cost**
16 July 2010	Worthing	London Victoria	Southern Rail	£4.25
16 July 2010	London Euston	Liverpool Lime Street	Virgin Rail	£26.00
17 July 2010	Liverpool	Douglas	Steam Packet Co.	£25.00
25 July 2010	Douglas	Liverpool	Steam Packet Co.	£25.00
25 July 2010	Liverpool Lime Street	London Euston	Virgin Rail	£19.00
25 July 2010	London Vitoria	Worthing	Southern Rail	£4.25
			Total	**£103.50**

Hotels

Date	Hotel	Town	Cost
16 July 2010	Travelodge	Liverpool	£47.00
17 July 2010	Ellan Vannin	Douglas	£40.00
18 July 2010	The George	Castletown	£40.40
19 July 2010	The Anchorage	Port Erin	£30.00
20 July 2010	The Waldick	Peel	£35.00
21 July 2010	Sulby Glen Hotel	Sulby	£35.00
22 July 2010	The Greaves	Laxey	£25.00
23 July 2010	Ellan Vannin	Douglas	£40.00
23 July 2010	Ellan Vannin	Douglas	£40.00
		Total	**£332.50**

Index

List of Illustrations

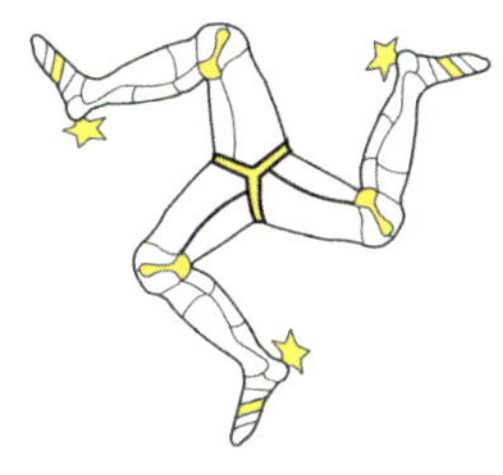

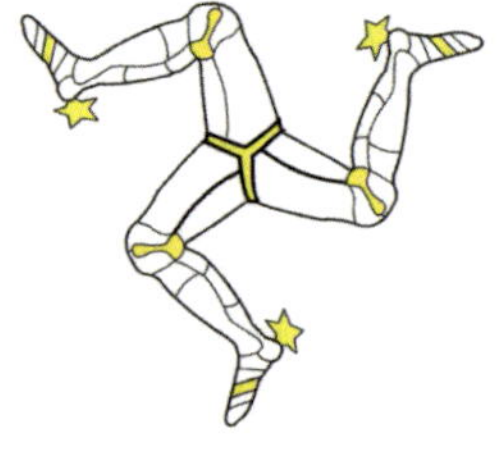

ND - #0263 - 080726 - C82 - 197/132/7 - PB - 9781780356587 - Gloss Lamination